concrete whalesong

ashley capes

concrete whalesong
Copyright Ashley Capes ©2025

Cover Art: Ashley and Christina P
Layout & Typset: Close-Up Books

All rights reserved. No part of this book may be reproduced in any form by any electronic or mechanical means including photocopying, recording, or information storage and retrieval without permission in writing from the authors.

ISBN-978-1-7636809-3-7

Published by Close-Up Books
Melbourne, Australia

Japan, 2024

acknowledgements

Some of the poems in this collection previously appeared on various social media platforms but additional pieces were first published (or are forthcoming) in:

seashores, failed haiku, haiku down under anthology, Kingfisher and *Modern Haiku.*

Thanks to the editors of the above publications for their support.

Above all, thank you to Rob Scott, whose advice and insights have been absolutely invaluable!

scattered blossoms
inside the taxi
everything is spotless

concrete whalesong

streetlight
pulling us toward
the next konbini

chopsticks scrape sushi alive on my tongue

go-kart fumes
climbing
the neon lighthouse

concrete whalesong

soft static –
bamboo brooms
in the park

toadstools stretching
for the sun
I ready pen and paper

Ashley Capes

watching me cross
the nightingale floor
CCTV

concrete whalesong

a flashing coin –
Zenigata Heiji
strikes again

shivering menus line the street Akihabara maids

Ashley Capes

        caged at the
        crosswalk –
        digital birds

rain over Osaka –
thunder patters
against the window

zigzagging
through the market
scent of meat

scattering butterflies
with every step
I watch for traffic

concrete whalesong

engine-oil-rainbow meets creeping green

empty shrine
I am left to
capture the wind

Ashley Capes

torii gate –
vending machines
in attendance

unable to recognise
my accent
cherry-sauce doughnut

concrete whalesong

cloud-soup
pink slithering
down from above

birthday wishes
keep shrinking
a good night's sleep

Arashiyama dawn –
bamboo and tourists
woven together

concrete whalesong

memory chips away each new photograph

spent leaves everywhere
the edge
of electric town

Ashley Capes

crossing the city
at 4am
concrete whalesong

concrete whalesong

hovering over
bicycles at rest –
old streetlight

pale shells
and pink blossoms
corpse of dawn

colours muted –
my inhaler echoes
between bamboo

somewhere
in Kyoto
I am finally nameless

concrete whalesong

lining up
for naginata practice –
wagtails in the park

snow-capped Mona Lisa Fuji-san is everywhere

nylon serpent leaves crying for rain

concrete whalesong

racing the clouds
to somewhere blue
shinkansen

empty threat
no bark to the
mosquito's whine

pouring into
the konbini
glistening umbrellas

spring breeze –
the scent of garbage
from two floors down

hearing aids sing
from the lobby
late for our taxi

my face pressed
against the glass
another cherry blossom!

concrete whalesong

scramble crossing pale flyers limited-time

giggling at the touch
of fishing line
Lake Saiko

concrete whalesong

basking in
the spring sun
golden pavilion

staring between leaves pale blue night

vanishing into
the morning light
birdsong

food-carts rattling
toward tomorrow –
the sky redlines

Thanks for reading!

The haiku and senryu within this collection were composed both during and right after a trip to Japan in the spring of 2024.

More haiku and senryu by Ashley:

orion tips the saucepan
old stone
teeth of the world

www.ingramcontent.com/pod-product-compliance
Lightning Source LLC
Chambersburg PA
CBHW030536080526
44585CB00014B/969